GODFREY HOLMES studied So[...]
and Psychology at the Universit[...] of Nottingham
and Manchester. He then taught [...] for a few years
in two Comprehensive Schools before entering
Social Work with young people, and families
at risk.

Godfrey Holmes is the author of four other books.
He has also written extensively for newspapers
and magazines. Twice he has been President
of Matlock Speakers Club.

Cover design by Mike Ring
of Inscribe Graphics

YOUR CONVERSATION – OR MINE?

Two Hundred Tactics When Talking

Godfrey H. Holmes

NETHERMOOR BOOKS

Published by:
Nethermoor Books, 32 Miriam Avenue, Somersall, Chesterfield, Derbyshire S40 3NF
01-246-566-069

ISBN 0 9536016 0 9

Design, typesetting & production: Country Books, Little Longstone, Derbyshire DE45 1NN
Printed & Bound by: MFP Design & Print, Stretford, Manchester M32 0JT
Cover origination by: GA Graphics, Stamford, Lincolnshire PE9 2RE

for

F. W. Peter Dawkins

Secretary, then National President

of the Association

of Speakers Clubs

The two hundred tactics when talking outlined in this book have been gathered from many sources over many years.

Whilst the author has been extremely careful to preserve the originality of this collection, he acknowledges that there will be published material somewhere covering some of the same ground.

CONTENTS:

INTRODUCTION

This book arose from my chance encounter with a lawyer. She was explaining what cross-examination in court means and what it aims to achieve.

She suggested I should never tell a barrister or judge more than *the bare minimum* required to answer any question put to me.

It would then be up to other parties to keep making suggestions or raising issues until they found out exactly what they needed to know.

In other words, I was to employ *a strategy* at the start of what could be a hostile exchange, and throughout.

It struck me that the best way to speak more **in all situations** might be to speak *less*.

There is hardly any comeback from omission. The other person still has the chance to find out more, depending.

This approach – if adopted in everyday conversation or "informal" meetings – does sound clinical, almost detached. Why use tactics when your object is spontaneity?

But the potential for gaining ground *still rests* with your colleagues, friends and adversaries. They know the rules. So why shouldn't you?

All through this book I use the word **conversation**. But these two hundred tactics can be transplanted into many (perhaps more formal) discussions and deliberations.

This book will succeed if otherwise drab, tired, or meandering conversations become enlightened and entertaining. Also if it gives people back the *initiative*.

At first, those you talk to will be startled – and a trifle suspicious. But these devices do work: alerting, prompting, monitoring, or deflecting the conversationalist. Talk freely.

+++++++++++++

HOW TO USE THIS BOOK

Do not try to read this book from cover to cover. That could he quite overwhelming. Instead:

- Dip into this book;

- Dip into it when you want an encounter to go well;

- Dip into it when you think an encounter went badly;

- Dip into it when you find a relationship is going nowhere – or worse, when it is going downhill;

- Return to this book whenever you need to.

Take a tactic and try it.

Rehearse the tactic and try it again.

Use a tactic first with close friends or family.
That is a safe environment.

Then try it at work, or when you have to make a complaint.
These settings are more difficult. You're far more likely to be
misunderstood.

Learn to be a tactician. *Tact* is part of being a tactician.
Ingenious strategies are risky.
No verbal contact, or contract, is ever going to be risk-free.

Prepare carefully for confrontations ahead.
You *will* make mistakes.
You will even get burnt setting conversation alight!
But there are rewards as well as penalties for being bold and imaginative.

- Never be discouraged;

- Never be distracted by the tactics of others;

- Never revert to previous form;

- And never give up.

Tactics can be tried again and again. What works in one setting flops in another. What succeeds in one setting can be adapted for a different setting.

"Failure" matters less because there are so many other and varied human contacts each day and each week to allow further experiment. Our lives are spent talking.

If you've unblocked communication as a partner, do it as a parent. If you've enhanced communication with a colleague, see if that's possible with somebody "higher up."

The great benefit of a book like this is your chance *to decode* conversation – to understand it better and to fear it less.

Know what attitude to take, what impact to make – and, most important of all, when to stop.

+++++++++++++++++++

A DEFINITION OF SETTINGS

CONVERSATION is only one of the available words for a one-to-one (or very small group) meeting. Here are the others. . . in alphabetical order :

ALTERCATION:	Hostile Meeting, Argument, Usu. 2 persons.
ARGUMENT:	As above.
ASSEMBLY:	Gathering for specific purpose. Usu. large.
AUDIENCE:	a) One-to-one meeting at either person's wish.
	b) Large gathering for set-piece presentation.
CHAT:	Intimate conversation. Very small number.
CONFAB.:	As above.
CONFERENCE:	Gathering for specific purpose. Usu. large.
CONFRONTATION:	Hostile meeting.Usu. 2 persons. Demonstration.
CONGREGATION:	Gathering for specific purpose. Usu. large.
CONGRESS:	Gathering usu.specific. Usu. large.
CONSULTATION:	One-to-one meeting. Discussion.
CONTEST:	Hostile meeting . Often one-to-one.
CONVENTION:	Gathering for specific purpose. Usu. large.
CONVERSATION:	Intimate chat, or gossip, or discussion. Small.
COUNCIL:	Meeting to reach a decision. Usu. large.

COUNSEL(LING):	One-to-one session to air problem areas.
CROSS-EXAMINATION:	Systematic testing of evidence. Usu.hostile.
DEBATE:	Discussion or testing of position. All sizes.
DELIBERATION:	Meeting to reach a decision. Usu. small.
DEMONSTRATION:	Meeting to reach understanding. Usu. hostile.
DIALOGUE:	One-to-one discussion. Talk.
DISCOURSE:	Meeting to present information.
DISCUSSION:	Informal debate. Sharing issues. Usu. small.
DISPUTE:	Hostile meeting. Often small.
ENCOUNTER:	General non-specific,unplanned, meeting. Small.
ENGAGEMENT:	One-to-one discussion for specific purpose.
EXAMINATION:	Systematic testing of position.Can be hostile.
GATHERING:	Large meeting, usu. for specific purpose.
GOSSIP:	Intimate exchange of information. Chat.
INTERROGATION:	Hostile testing of evidence. One-to-one.
INTERVIEW:	a) Any one-to-one meeting granted;
	b) One person confronted for job or opportunity for evidence.
MEETING:	Any gathering, large or small. Often business.
PARTY:	Informal gathering for fun and chatter.
PRESENTATION:	Specific meeting to present a case.

RALLY:	Large gathering to demonstrate or make a case.
RE-UNION:	Specific meeting for chat and re-acquaintance.
SEMINAR:	Organized (small) gathering for business.
SESSION:	Fixed-length meeting. Usu. large.
SUPERVISION:	One-to-one meeting to discuss work & progress.
TALK:	a) One-to-one discussion. Chat.
	b) Organized presentation of information.
TETE-A-TETE:	Very informal one-to-one encounter. Gossip.
UNBURDENING:	Ventilation.
UNION:	Usu. very large convention. Demonstration.
VENTILATION:	Usu. one-to-one unburdening of a problem.
WORKSHOP:	Small group discussion for business.
WRANGLE:	Hostile one-to-one encounter.

200
TACTICS
WHEN
TALKING:

ALL

Be especially aware of anyone who starts a statement or a conversation with the word "ALL . . ." eg:

● "All doctors are agreed . . . ,"

● "All the evidence suggests . . . ," or

● "All your work is shoddy and careless."

You do not have to look far to find an **exception**. If there were not exceptions to rules, laws, and research, most lawyers would be out of a job.

Ask for the exception. Better still, *supply* the exception.

AND . . .

And is a beautiful word. Grammar books used to discourage children from starting a sentence with **and**.

Nowadays, **and** is more accepted everywhere.

The best **and** is the over-emphasised **and** . . .
- "... **and** I would like some turnips, **and** some carrots."
- "**and** I want your signature, **and** I want your identity number, **and** I want a receipt. . ."

Used like this, **and** is obviously infuriating. Soon the And-person is being booted out of the room.

Sometimes, attempt a blind **and** midway through someone's hesitant story or explanation. Quizically say "**And**?"

BUT

Just as there are some people with a problem for every solution, so there are others with a BUT for every affirmation.

- "...but that's not possible,"

- "...but there will be strong opposition,"

- "but there's a snag": these are only three of three thousand BUTs.

Some "positive" up-and-coming managers even say: "I'll accept no Buts!"

Now, there *is* a tactic worth remembering.

CONFIDENTIALLY

Confidentiality does not just mean the ability to keep a secret. Confidentiality is also *a style* of dealing with other people:

- "Between you and me. . ."

- "Just between ourselves. . ."

- "You can trust me with what you are about to say. . ." or:

- "I am sharing this with you, specially, because. . ."

Confidentiality often accompanies whispering. The listener feels that (s)he is the most privileged person in the entire world.

DON'T

I once had a friend who could simply say: "Don't!" and people would stop in their tracks.

Most of us need to add something else, such as:

- "Don't say that!"
- "Don't try it!" or
- "Don't mess me about!'
- "Don't look so mardy!"

Don't is quite a powerful, and daunting instruction. It works by catching the respondent in a state of surprise.

CERTAINLY

Distrust anyone who says: "Certainly . . ." too often.
There are only one or two certainties in life.

People say "Certainly . . ." as a favour, in acknowledgement, or to
signal a level of agreement.

Beware of: "It is certainly the case that . . ." or
"We are certain to face . . ."

"Certainly . . ." is all too frequently followed by a snag, a
qualification, or a disappointment.

FINALLY . . .

"Finally," or : "And Finally. . ." are excellent ways to draw discussion to a close.

The other person(s) may or may not understand that time is at a premium. Time may, indeed, not be at a premium!

Saying: "Finally. . ." draws proceedings to a close. "Finally. . ." is also the cue that you have nearly finished saying all you intended to say.

The trick then is to drone on and on despite having said "Finally. . ." The word: "Lastly. . ." is just as effective.

FRANKLY . . .

People start by saying: "Frankly . . ." when they have no intention whatever of being frank or open.

The endorsement: "Frankly . . ." makes the listener **expect** a very frank statement or assessment of the situation.

"Frankly . . ." is therefore a mislabelling, on most occasions.

Very few people can afford to be completely frank. Frankness means risk, an unwelcome transparency.

So only use : "Frankly . . ." if your name is Frank.

GOSH

I have a friend who says: "Gosh! after even the most mundane anecdote or observation.

And it is amazingly effective.

The speaker is not expecting a "Gosh!" What (s)he is saying simply does not merit a "Gosh!"

As might be deduced, "Gosh!" cannot work if completely rigged. 'Gosh!" must be well-intentioned.

HISTORICALLY . . .

"Historically," or: "Historically speaking. . ." are both valued additions to any debate. "Historically" is sufficiently woolly to allow no come-back.

It matters not one little bit that historically no lesson was learnt; no such thing happened, or that historically *the opposite* conclusion can be drawn.

"Historically. . ." sounds grand enough to authenticate whatever is being said. Listeners do not ask for chapter and verse; and if they do, history is divided on the subject.

NO

Enjoy the word "**no**."

Unlike its cousin: "**yes**", the word "**no**" is bold. . . and almost beyond challenge.

"**No**" sounds nice and decisive. It needs no expansion nor explanation. "**No**" is definitive — hated especially by argumentative children.

Listeners soon have to give up or disappear.

OBJECTIVELY SPEAKING

"Objectively speaking . . ." sounds a rather grand — and certainly a reliable — way to start a sentence.

Unfortunately, it is extremely difficult for a human speaker to be "objective," even on a matter of fact.

"He was one of those involved in a pile-up" — is open to lots of interpretations or eye-witness accounts. Objectivity is restricted to the victim's age and address, not much more.

Humans are, by definition, **subjective**: so they are better starting most sentences: "Subjectively speaking . . ." At least the listener is not then caught unawares.

PASS

Any longlasting TV programme is almost bound to leave an addition to the language. So it was with MASTERMIND and the response : "**Pass**." "Pass!" was a quick way for the contestant to say: "I cannot remember," or "I do not know the right answer." If an acquaintance or a work colleague asks you something awkward, simply reply: "**Pass!**"

POINT TAKEN

"Point taken!" is yet another veiled put-down when you have been bombarded with arguments you do not necessarily agree with.

"Point taken!" shuts down the conversation without causing undue offence. And it leaves open the possibility that the point might never again be seriously taken up or adhered to.

The point is merely absorbed:
"The Government should pass a law. . ." "Point taken!"

RIGHT

We all know people who put certain key phrases into every sentence: "To be quite honest," or "You know what I mean?"

Such links check out the listener's understanding, or hope to make him listen more intently. In some parts of the country, it is common to add the word: "Right" to every sentence, or every part of every sentence." **"Right"** is useful because it can be drawn in by speaker or listener.

If employed only occasionally, "Right" can be quite arresting.

TRUE

A sure conversation-stopper is the word: "True."

Try it.

It does not matter whether the preceding opinion or observation is the least bit true.

"True!" will still shut the other person down.

WELL SAID

"Well said!" is an ingenious device to build into any discussion, particularly where you're heading for dispute or rancour.

"Well said!" does not really require any amplification. It is a compliment, doubtless a well-meant compliment, which listener(s) can take any way they wish.

Who knows?: the original speaker might feel quite chuffed – and drop guard when your own quite contentious views follow.

YES, AND . . .

"YES, and. . ." is actually quite dismissive. This sequence *sounds* as if it is being helpful, but moves a discussion or negotiation on rather *too* quickly.

A distinct impression is given that the other person's contribution was neither very important nor listened to.

The second person, the person saying: "Yes, and. . ." only wants to hear the sound of his or her own voice.

● "Millie won £50 on her premium bond." "Yes, and I won £180 in last Wednesday's Lottery."

● "I've just bought 2 chairs." "Yes, and my new suite is in leather."

YES, YES, YES

"Yes, yes, yes!" is a classic sign of impatience.

- ● "Yes, yes, yes!" reveals somebody in an unseemly haste to get onto the next point, or to catch the next bus.

- ● "Yes, yes, yes!" like all potential put-downs can be rehearsed or exaggerated.

- ● "Yes, yes, yes!" – however irate or irritating – allows for precious little comeback.

Except that a very brave soul could reply:
"It's all very well and good saying: 'Yes, yes, yes!' but have you really understood what I've been trying to say?"

ALLITERATION

Alliteration is the art of starting most words in one sentence with the same letter:

- ● "Look! Listen! Learn! is what I say;"

- ● "Put Peter's piggy-bank back on the pot-shelf! or

- ● "Be back before bed-time, Benjamin, or there'll be trouble."

Therefore alliteration has something in common with both poetry and speaking in staccato.

There is a high chance that alliteration will sound artificial and forced. To avoid this, keep intentioned alliteration to prepared slogans like: "Find Food First."

CONTRIVED EXCLAMATION

The contrived exclamation, like any other talking tactic, has to be used very sparingly. The contrivance lies more in the slightly sarcastic or overdone *tone of voice* than the actual words used.

"Really!" is an example of a comment that could easily be misinterpreted. "Jolly!" and "Golly!" are sisters.

The most commonly contrived exclamations are blasphemous, swearing, or both: "Jeepers Creepers!" being an obvious variation of Jesus Christ, as is "Crikey."

"Bingo!" in one contrived exclamation I enjoy. Psychologists say that an outrageous "A-a-a-a-gh!" or "G e e e !" moves people on when what is being discussed has hit a rut, or indifference.

MANY A GIGGLE

Think about introducing a giggle into some of your funnier – or not so funny – observations and reminiscences.

In the past, you might have been irritated by giggly voices – but the impact of a suppressed giggle on your listener is quite marked.

The listener pays more attention, because (s)he is grateful for being allowed somewhere normally closed off.

Giggling lightens the **tone** of what is being said, without necessarily sounding frivolous.

AN UPTURNED VOICE

Try ending each sentence by slightly raising instead of lowering the voice (trailing off).

People hardly expect an **upbeat** end to a sentence which otherwise would have ended on a **downbeat** or defeatist note.

So always leave your listener clinging to your last word(s).

They will be a lot happier because *you* are obviously a lot happier.

WHISPER IN MY EAR

Whispering need not be inaudible. Whispers can be shrill or soft, urgent or reassuring. All speaking should incorporate pitch, as well as pause and pace.

Dropping to a whisper acts to increase confidentiality; or – strangely – it adds to the immediacy of what has to be said.

Whispering allows for a whole range of emotions. But do use whisper sparingly.

STACCATO VOICE

The Italians were great inventors of ways to describe voice modulation of modification: lentamente, forte, diminuendo, crescendo, staccato.

The staccato voice has a rough edge. Staccato means splitting long words into several syllables, dwelling on those syllables for less than half a second, or letting syllables collide:

- "I-will-be-ratt-ling-on-his-door;"
- "Th-i-s-i-s-my-in-str-u-c-sh-un;" or
- "I-yam-mask-king-gAnd-drew-to . . ."

Staccato can be varied further to go high/low/high/low. Good at times.

THE UNDERTAKER SPEAKING

Learn how to speak in the style of voice exactly **opposite** to what the situation demands. Say something serious in a light, instead of a cheerless, voice. Then: say something happy and informative in grave tones.

Two examples are : "I'm afraid our manager is leaving," said joyously, or :"Jenny has just found out she's won the lottery," spoken solemnly.

The purpose of this tactic is **surprise**, not tease; so contradictory tone of voice should only be brought into conversation or announcement on rare occasions.

SINGING

Generally, we pigeonhole people and occasions. We know that Sylvia will always squeak, and Jeremy always thunder. We also know that whispering is for churches, shouting for noisy discotheques.

So we can easily throw a listener into confusion by changing this acceptable way of communicating without any warning. For instance, when a mother is chiding a naughty 4-year old child, what better than to sing (or almost sing):

"This is *the last*; this is *the last*; chance Ricky;
Chance Ricky gets. . . before beddy-byes, bedby-byes"?

Singing gets a message across swiftly and effectively.

CHANTING

Chanting is another technique taken out of the concert hall, or the choir-stalls. Sometimes it is called Choral Speaking when it is done in unison.

There is nothing wrong with using chanting in everyday speech.

A good impersonator can even replicate how a chant might sound in chapel or on the football terrace.

Chanting is excellent for **repetition**, eg. "Finish this silly talk; finish this silly talk Now; "or for gaining pace in an important message: "50 is to-day's target, 60 to-morrow; 50 Sunday; Sixty Monday."

VAST AUDIENCE

We have all met people who play to the gallery. . . but not usually in very small rooms, or intimate situations.

The great advantage of speaking *as if* to a vast audience is *expansiveness*; also an added air of authority.

Some listeners find it intimidating to see a tub-thumper only a few feet away [and tub-thumping in any case should only be used very rarely] but the trick here is *to lower the voice* at exactly the same time as exaggerating hand gestures and looking over and above listeners; indeed, looking round eagerly at non-existent bodies.

TAP, TAP, TAP

Tapping feet, or tapping table during conversation is very rude --
but it makes a point. Strumming, or drumming, makes the same
point.

All tapping is a sign of restlessness. As such, it should be counted as
non-vocal communication.

Floor and table are not the only near noise-producers. Pen-tapping
is common, finger-clicking less so.
Knocking anything against a china cup or a glass pane adds to
resonance.

Tapping drives people up the wall.

GAZING UP AT THE CEILING

Gazing up at the ceiling is so forbidden that in all arenas of authority: court, police station, employment, school etc., gazers are openly reprimanded. So gazing up at the ceiling is usually not an option.

In debate or informal conversation, however, gazing up at the ceiling – though infuriating – is allowed by default.

Does it signal boredom? Or does it signal contempt? What is so fascinating about the ceiling? Is the ceiling beautifully decorated? Is the deity up there?

STARING

Staring is a culturally sensitive as well as socially delicate tool in conversation. Then there is *the gender* angle.

If you stare at somehody, they will soon look away. It is a taboo to outstare somebody, beyond childhood.

Some people maintain firm eye-contact when speaking, but look away when listening. Others maintain the eye-contact for the listening but find it hard to raise so much as glance whilst talking. Anybody who does not understand your background could be offended. All people who have been terrorised in childhood find adult eye-contact exacting.

Staring at any woman is probably intimidating.

SMALL-TALK

The very title: "small-talk" is patronizing and dismissive. The term belongs to the days of the (with) drawing room, where men would talk politics and business whilst their womenfolk occupied themselves with inconsequential gossip.

But, like all extremes, small-talk does have some value. Small-talk is best used *to lubricate* a discussion — especially one that may turn out quite painful or contentious.

Therefore, it is better to talk of cricket before criticism, and knitting before the nitty-gritty.

HOBBY TALK

Hobby talk is simply the commonest example of small-talk.

If your hobby is painting, comment on the pictures up on another person's wall. If your hobby is stamp-collecting, comment on the stamp that decorates the envelope.

Hobby talk is a loosener. Particularly, football! It is also very irritating to the *non*-hobbyist or to the person who wants to get straight to the heart of the matter.

Of course, among like-minded hobbyists, hobby talk is actually the principal talk and needs no justification.

HE SAID, SHE SAID

Because the words "He" and "She" rhyme, and because they are
direct alternatives, (also because they underline gender), they sound
good in the same sentence or pair of sentences:

- "He said this: . . . but *She* said: . . .";
- "He went to Rome, but *She* went to Florence":
- "He chose jelly; *She* chose ice-cream."

It is absolutely essential that the 'he' comes before the 'she'.

Even where real names are known, he did/she did contrasts better
than Cuthbert did/ Rosanna did.

HAVE YOU HEARD?

In the corner of every office, school, or market-place people are asking: "Have you heard. . ?"

With the revolution in mass communication: phones, cables, channels and sources of information, the question: "Have you heard. . ?" will either gain or lose its relevance. Certain it is that there will be less *shared experience* before that crucial question is asked and answered.

"Have you heard. . ?" is a marvellous way of gaining listeners' attention, drawing them in.

BEEN THERE, DONE THAT

At the end of the 1990s it became trendy to say: "Been there, done that!" – or a variation like: "I've seen the film and bought the video and worn the tee-shirt. . ."

The impact is the same: *dismissiveness.*

Such dismissiveness squashes the enthusiasm of another speaker who really had stumbled upon something original to add or to to recall.

Multi-media and global experiences are now much cheaper and more accessible than ever before – hence our difficulty arousing much excitement.

I AM UNHAPPY

To say: "I am unhappy" is — paradoxically – happy. Nobody can possibly challenge the statement : "I am unhappy," because there is no way one person can tell for sure that another person *is* unhappy.

The device: "I am unhappy" is especially useful when discussion or conversation takes a turn for the worse, or to your disadvantage.

"I am unhappy" is a statement best *not* elaborated upon.Then the other person has the responsibility for dropping the subject, or altering their viewpoint.

I'M DREAMING

Dreams would crop up more in day-to-day speech if only a crooner had not sung: "I'm dreaming of a White Christmas!" also if the image of psychoanalysis had not been lying on some couch waiting to have one's dreams unravelled.

To say: "I'm dreaming. . ." is to bring about wish fulfilment without having to be *fully committed* to what you most want.

To say: "I'm dreaming. . ." is a good excuse for having misheard something, or having forgotten something that was requested.

Needless to say, you shouldn't dream and drive.

I'M REMEMBERING

The words: "I Remember, I Remember," are very powerful. Remembrance is so important that we have remembrance gardens, remembrance books and remembrance days.

To start a conversation with a memory, or to draw in a recovered memory somewhere during its course, enriches that conversation.

The memory can be of a book or a newspaper article. A memory can be second-hand, *converted to first-hand*. Or your memory can be entirely fictional! No one knows better.

WHEN I WAS A BOY [A GIRL] . . .

Although it nearly always raises a groan, the introduction: "When I was a boy. . ." or "When I was a girl. . ." is surprisingly effective.

Again, there is no earthly way the listener can authenticate what is about to be said. So, although it is hackneyed, the speaker can use the cringe-factor to his or her own advantage.

After all, there are many hackneyed phrases in everyday conversation which would not be used (or over-used) if they did not have some merit.

I'VE ACTUALLY SEEN IT

Capping is a useful tool in conversation. We can cap by drawing discussion to an abrupt conclusion, by interrupting once too often, by leaving the room, or by coming out with a final flourish.

One of the best final flourishes is to say: "Well, I've actually **seen** it."

There are not many replies to such clear testimony. To have been there, seen it allows little room for argument.

How about borrowing a first-hand sighting from someone else?

AND HOW DID YOU RESPOND?

The table-tennis of everyday conversation can be played second hand:

> "Mary refused to come shopping with me."
> "And how did you respond?"
> "I threw the shopping list straight in the bin."
> "And how did she respond?"

This tactic moves a story along more quickly.

Another name for "And how did you respond?" is *co-operative story-telling*, because the listener is urging the narrator on . . . willy-nilly.

LAST CLAUSE FIRST

No counselling course in social work or adult education would be complete without suggesting Last Clause First.

The idea here is always to pick up on the respondent's most recent observation before asking more. For instance:

> B: "I am so frightened of dogs barking."
> A: "Dogs barking. What about drills?"
> B: "They're frightening, but jets overhead are worst."
> A: "Low-flying jets. You are obviously unsettled."

Last Clause First is irritating – and contrived. Feasible, nonetheless, if only to show you are listening.

SPEAKING IN THE THIRD PERSON

If we use the words "He," "She," or "They," in everyday speech, we expect these people *not* to be in the room.

"Pat cannot be serious!" sounds different from
"You cannot be serious!"
"Your boss is asking . . . " – or "Your wife is wanting . . . "
both sound different from: "*I* am asking," "*I* want."

Try speaking in the third person whilst all are still in the room.

You will sound quite aggrieved when you say:
"I trusted *my friend* to . . . "

THREE STATEMENTS

One statement is significant. Three statements are thrice as significant. The number 3 is a natural and poetical ingredient of conversation or examination:

- past/present/future,
- yesterday/to-day/tomorrow,
- for/against/abstention, or
- left/right/middle.

We almost expect three of anything, particularly three reasons:
"You *Must* go to school:
first, because you'll meet lots of other chi]dren;
second, because you'll learn all your lessons;
third, because you've got to have your Dinner." *Four* points rarely work.

PUNCHLINE

No joke or narrative or reportage is complete without a punchline: a final line to sum everything up.

Some jokers and storytellers have the gift of building up to a punchline; others forget the line or let it tail off.

The best punchline in any conversation is carefully prepared *and rehearsed*. Many radio and TV correspondents actually make up their punchlines first, then build up to that point in increments. The punchline is what you want everyone else to remember hours or days later.

Other names for the punchline are "mouth-shot" or "sound-bite."

WHO? WHAT? WHEN? WHERE? WHY?

These five words are variously described as the five tenets of journalism, the five elements of storytelling, or the five soldiers of speech.

Answering all five questions gives the fullest picture possible. People know the event, and its repercussions.

In a tight situation, demanding to know:
"Who? What? When? Where? Why?" can sound fairly –
or unfairly – intimidating.

Try asking them in a different order, or *indirectly*.

SIMILE

Hardly an hour of the day goes past before we resort to simile.

Simile depends on two different links: "Like a . . . ,' or "Just as . . . "

- "Money flowing like water;"
- "Weeping just like a tap;"
- "Yorkshire Pudding tasting just like leather;"
- "Circling as a cloud."

Similes are picturesque. One description merges effortlessly with another. Attention is gained through association.

METAPHOR

Metaphor is another figure of speech employed so often that millions of speakers who do not even know the word "metaphor" are using it!

- "He's carrying the world's worries on his shoulders."
- "They dared to give us a broom-cupboard and call it a single bedroom!"
- or: "Coffee break's a real oasis in these talks,"

are all examples of metaphor enriching speech.

In everyday conversation it is better *not to labour* the metaphor nor to search for it too diligently. Just reach out for whatever image comes to mind, and use it creatively.

PARABLE

The second-most famous parable is of a sower spreading his seeds on rough ground, stony ground, pathway, among weeds — or in fertile soil. Just like a teacher trying to teach a class of unsettled school-children!

That is the nature of a parable: a railway where one track is the story, the parallel track the underlying meaning.

Talking in parables is now rather out of fashion, but it works.

A parable does not even have to be a lengthy. The pensioner constantly refurbishing and re-ordering the humble wooden shed at the bottom of his garden has obvious parallels.

TAUTOLOGY

Tautology is really a sealed argumnent — where the end is justified by the beginning or the beginning by the end:

- "Punishment is harsh because it hurts the offender;"or
- "Horror films harm children because they are left upset;"or
- "Fatty foods fail by causing obesity."

Too much of anything is bad. But further proof is needed than that harm leads to further harm. There are always exceptions.

More important, there are complications along the path between cause and effect. Singletons are happy for other reasons than that they are not married.

MYSTERY

Most speech tells a story; and the more *mystery* there is in that story, the better. People listen to mysteries more attentively than dull platitudes and inevitabilities.

I had not fully appreciated mystery in speech until, first, I heard a performance poet on radio unravelling one; and second, I saw a choir on television singing: "God move in a mysterious way." And they actually sung it mysteriously.

Mystery is a bit like confidentiality in speech. . . trading on the imagination, and the unfathomable.

WHAT WOULD YOU SAY IF?

Imagine a point has been argued, and no clear conclusion has been reached. There is good faith on both sides or on all sides. Someone must move matters on.

This is where: "What would you say if . . . ?" comes in:

- "What would you say to 9 on a weekday, 10 at weekends?"
- "What would you say if we stopped cows, kept sheep?"
- "What would you say if the newlyweds were expecting?"

There is no harm flying a kite. Nobody loses face. Nor is anyone committed before they are ready.

THE BIRDS ARE SINGING . . .

"The birds are singing; the lambs are playing; the sun is shining. . .
and the coach will take another 3 hours to repair."

Some of the best jokes are over-used. This joke lightens the burden
of unwelcome news. Again it is a tool of suspense (or indeed, of
repose).

A well-known variation is:
"All systems are in place; all employees are happy at their stations;
all paperwork is despatched. . . BUT. . ."

DO YOU WANT THE GOOD NEWS FIRST?

Terribly hackneyed it might be, but it always raises a laugh.
The question: "Do you want the good news first?" –
or alternatively "Do you want the bad news first?"
is really a wind-up. It is a way of gaining the listener's full attention;
also of heightening the suspense.

"The good news is that I got the job! The bad news is that I'm only
going to be paid half what I am now."

THAT'S GOOD

Many a comedy sketch has benefited from the (seemingly positive) remark: **"That's good!"** –
whereupon the narrator relates something that is clearly less welcome, prompting: **"That's bad!"** –
and so on.

The beauty of: **"That's good!"** is that it not only indicates you have been listening; it also helps the first speaker enter the inevitable qualification.

EMBELLISHMENT

One of the secrets of story-telling is Embellishment – the addition of details not originally there.

Embellishment occurs spontaneously when we recall past events; and especially when we recount past dialogue for the benefit of somebody who has not heard it all before.

Embellishment can be *authentic*, in that it adheres to the spirit of what took place, if not the letter.

Use this tactic selectively. Avoid getting a reputation.

SPEAKING AS A . . .

Annoying it certainly is. And rather smug. But: "Speaking, as a mother. . ," or: "Speaking as a manager. . ." or: "Speaking as a missionary. . ." adds quite a lot of credence to what is being said.

Those who promote themselves in this way need not fear contradiction. Patently they are whom they say they are.

Whatever opinion or statement or judgment follows is probably fairly banal. Even a famous politician or future king can sound humdrum. But they are: "Speaking as an expert . . ."

SPEAKING AS A FRIEND OF . . .

"Speaking as a friend [associate] of. . ." sounds outrageous and it is open to some comeback. What constitutes a friend? What constitutes a colleague ?

Theoretically, everybody who works for Marks and Spencer is a colleague of the Chief Executive; and everybody who works for B.B.C. is able to speak on behalf of the Director General!

Name-dropping has always peppered conversation. But in a job interview, acquaintanceship can rebound. Speak for yourself.

TELL ME MORE

There is good psychology in saying: "Tell me more!"

It's always worth hearing a bit more than you have heard already. That's the means for an interviewer or a conversationalist testing out what more is on offer.

"Tell me more!" is also a brilliant alternative to the much derided *direct* question (which cramps the other person's style): eg. "What did you feel?" or "Are you attached?"

On the other hand, said in the wrong tone of voice: "Tell me more!" sounds a little sarcastic, as if the original observation is not entirely believed.

WHAT DO YOU THINK?

Tennis players and table-tennis players keep lobbing the ball in an opponent's direction.

So it is with conversation, and that other tactic: "What are you trying to say?"

The allied question: "What do you think?" is quite fundamental.

Traditionally, this question has been asked *after* one person in a conversation or debate has said what (s)he thinks. But there is no reason why a questioner should not also be challenged with that questioner's own question:
"What do **you** think?" — to get the ball rolling.

YOU WERE SAYING?

"You were saying?" is a very useful line in conversation, linking something said a few minutes ago, with something still needing to be said.

Again, this is a tool that avoids the dreaded direct question. It keeps a conversation moving.
"You were saying?" is especially appropriate after an interruption, somebody coming in or going out.

"You were saying?" can also mark *the end* of a conversation because the first person might well reply:
"Oh! It wasn't really important . . ."

WHO ARE YOU?

The introductory question: "Who are you?" is so simple that most people imagine it is being used routinely. . . it is not.

Maybe somebody in the room has forgotten a name, or a face, or a previous meeting – and is too embarrassed to say so.
Maybe a participant cannot hack the re-union. Memories are all at sea; yet clarification comes across as insulting.

Alternatively, a silent man's presence in the room will not be clear; is he boyfriend, neighbour, brother, -ex?

The more aggressive question: "Who are *you* to. . . ?" can be employed to undermine *the legitimacy* of someone's contribution in addition to its origin.

YOU SHOULD BE . . .

"**You should be** . . ." can be used in many ways – most of them unhelpful :

- "You should be glad,"
- "You should be grateful,"
- "You should be more attentive," – or, fulsomely:
- "You should be in politics,"
- "You should turn professional,"
- "You should not be so low down the pecking-order."

The beauty (or misery) of "**You should be** . . ." is that it allows very little comeback. It's not really a compliment, and it's wretchedly patronizing, but it *sounds* well- intentioned.

The only possible reply is: "Don't tell *me*. . ."

YOU WILL BE FEELING . . .

"You will be feeling . . . " is potentially the most insensitive and intrusive observation of all.

There is no way Callum can accurately measure what Diane is feeling or thinking – or how she has felt or thought in the past.

Callum robs Diane by *even pretending* to guess how she feels.

"I know how you feel . . . " is even worse, even where Callum thinks he has been through a similar ordeal to Diane's.

YOU ARE OBVIOUSLY ANGRY

"You are obviously angry" – is a ludicrous statement. It tells the listener (or respondent) nothing (s)he did not know already. At the same time it deflates his or her ability to be truly angry.

The angriest response to: "You are obviously angry" comes *from the person who was not angry in the first place*!

Nobody wants to be patronized.

"Would it make you less angry if. . ?" – now that's a different story.

COULD YOU LEAVE US?

"Could you leave us?" is a request most used in formal interviews and discussions.

"Could you leave us?" is also forbiddingly used in quasi-disciplinary proceedings.

"Could you leave us?" is a none-too-subtle way of getting rid of a child so that adults can discuss something on their own.

"Could you leave us?" is a snub – in some cases, the final snub – a put-down to the intruder.

BOMBSHELL

The bombshell is a bit like the exit-statement. Except that the bombshell can be used at any point between start and finish of a conversation or interview.

Bombshells need to be carefully premeditated and rehearsed.

If a bombshell is dropped spontaneously, it may be dropped too soon or too late. Some practitioners believe in the art of dropping the bombshell *at the very start of* a discussion. That forecloses a discussion. The discussion cannot go on.

All controversy is bomb-like: tossed in, to explode.

THAT'S ALL RIGHT JACK/JACQUELINE

People are amazingly responsive to their Christian names, or to their forenames. Anybody brought up much before 1960 would have used – or allowed other people to use – their first names less routinely than nowadays.

Even so: the first of one's names – or the most intimate has astonishing drawing power. That applies as much to the Susans as to the Paulettes. It is as if we will do almost anything for anyone who bothers to address us personally.

COULD I ASK YOUR ADVICE?

Collaring somebody for advice – asking for their opinion is a form of flattery. It is also very deceptive.

There is no guarantee the advice will be respected or followed; and the same advice could haunt the giver of it for years to come. Asking advice is, then, a trap.

The best response is to say: "I have little more to add," or, better still: "This can be said in favour. . , and this can be said against. . ."

FLATTERY

Flattery is different from flirting. Flattery need not have sexual undertone or overtone.

The flatterer is a smoothy, smoothing over rifts or wounds, preparing the way for a comment or a stance that may well be divisive or hurtful.

Flattery only works because the hearer [or object] of flattery cannot be quite sure whether it is sincere or deceptive.

ENCROACHING ON PERSONAL SPACE

People generally value the space around them. An illustration is the discomfort caused by shadowing somebody: literally, following in their shadow.

The circle of floor-space around somebody is sacrosanct. Only in exceptional foreseeable situations like a crowded pub, or a packed tube train is it permissible to encroach upon this space. To do so deliberately during conversation might appear wilful. . . but it gets a message across. Encroachment is most effective when the person of *lower status* dares to take the point right up to the person of perceived higher status.

SITTING TO SPEAK

The opposite of standing to speak is quite consciously choosing *to sit* in order to speak.

This action might well confuse the listener, because stance is a mark of status as well as introduction.

Sitting down [beguilingly] gives a note of informality, chattiness, where there is quite a harsh or unwelcome message to convey.

Sitting **next** to the listener rather than **opposite** makes the episode even less confrontational. But be aware: you are taking up somebody's personal space.

STANDING TO SPEAK

Body language is the essential ingredient of effective speech.
Nowhere is this more important than the action of standing to
address an audience, even an audience of one. Lecturers and
lawyers stand, as do teachers and some doctors.

It does not matter even if standing has *not* been given leave.

Many a soap opera on TV depends on the actor standing up at a
crucial moment, exasperated enough to leave the room, *then*
delivering the best lines.

BACK-TO-BACK

Sitting back-to-back, rather than facing, is a rarely adopted position for discussion — yet it is wonderfully effective.

Back-to-back talk defuses all tension. One or other party will sooner or later crumble and give in. One or both will be creased up with laughter.

So: after a period of tension, try talking back-to-back.

HEAD-IN-HANDS

Head-in-hands is possibly the most powerful gesture ever known to humankind. It is completely unfathomable, completely unanswerable.

Once that head is in those hands, does it signal tiredness, crying, despair, anxiety, bafflement, or embarrassment?
In a meeting of any kind, head-in-hands says: "can't play," "won't play," "don't play," or "I've played and lost" ?

Opinion is divided as to whether the burier of head in hands gets away with it. More than one child has actually had her hands clawed back from the head – so provocative is the display.

Essentially, the head cradled in the hands is *a ritual*: ritual steeped in emotional blackmail.

KNEADING OF THE HANDS

Kneading of the hands during a discussion or interview or argument is taken to be a classic sign of *anxiety*.

Hands can be clasped left/right, right/left; or they can be held/unheld in frequent succession. Hands can also be rubbed together as if in relish; or else each hand can quickly be enfolded round the other hand, without clear sequence.

Like all gestures, kneading of the hands can be casual, ritualistic, or false (in order to baffle the other person).

And there is not a lot of mileage in objecting.

THUMBS

The thumb is not the most significant part of the body until it is used in conversation.

Thumb up is a rather old-fashioned way of giving assent. Thumb down is still a jocular way of disagreeing rarely used one-to-one.

Twiddling thumbs indicates boredom in conversation.
Sucking thumbs points to an unanswered question, or sheer boredom.

TURNING TOWARD IN ORDER TO SPEAK

Frequently, we are not actually facing the person(s) we are addressing. This might he choice or accident, from shyness or even fear. A pre-planned seating arrangement [round a conference or wedding table] might make direct communication tricky.

The less it is possible, the more dramatic is the act of turning the whole body (or head) round to address one special individual in a group, or across the floor.

Don't hesitate to exaggerate this movement.

TURNING AWAY IN ORDER TO SPEAK

It is a risk – but sometimes a risk worth taking – actually to turn away from somebody whilst speaking to them.

This is an indication straightway:
- that the message is going to be unpalatable, or
- that the speaker is in a great hurry to get away, or
- that the status of the listener is inferior, or – finally –
- that the speaker is rather afraid of the listener.

Use with care.

KEEPING DISTANCE

Just as sitting or standing too close to somebody is often threatening, so is sitting or standing too far away.

We have all met characters who stand as near to the door as possible whilst speaking. It is almost as if they are opting out of proceedings. . . which is exactly what might be their intention.

Conversely, in some formal interviews, interviewees are sometimes *asked to* sit the furthermost length from their interviewers.
This enhances the status of the questioner(s), and increases tension.

Distance can actually *loosen* tongues.

FUNNY FACE

Because the face is so important in conversation, the muscles of the face can be flexed to meet any occasion, or to contradict any occasion (as with, most famously, the disingenuous smile).

Children pull funny faces – out of excitement or experiment. Adults can use this same trick.

Often, the "altered" face is a frown, a grimace, or a cheesy grin. Less usually, it can be a tightening of the chin, a pursing of the lips, a pouting of the lips, a screwing up of the cheeks. . . or any combination.

The lower lip can be withdrawn *completely*, to reveal a line of upper teeth. Watch the impact.

FORMING THE BODY INTO A SHAPE

This technique is adopted from the world of modern dance, but is also familiar to generations of Primary School children.

The body can be formed into a tree, a voting cross, a banana, a Christian cross, a hill or a hall stand (to list but a few shapes).

Most commonly in hostile situations, human bodies become just that: bodies. The subject swoons, or faints, or simply lies prostrate – as if unable to carry on.

THE DROPPED JAW

Because we are so used to seeing the dropped jaw in comedy, in sport, in the theatre, and in advertizing, seeing the dropped jaw in everyday conversation hardly surprises.

Traditionally, the jaw drops when news or excitement is too difficult to absorb.

The beauty of this gesture is that it is easily imitated or exaggerated – so much that hardly anybody believes in the jaw dropping except in jest.

Try lowering the jaw *very gradually*.

OOZING CONFIDENCE

In a more formal conversation or interview, it is possible to be a bag of nerves, yet still to speak with conviction and confidence.

The confident manner is like a lid on a saucepan. The lid is all the outsider sees, hiding the pan's contents.

The person who oozes confidence, even when his or her case is weak, throws the other party off-balance.

Sales people are especially good at sounding confident. However, a small leap from confidence brings stridency. And that arouses alienation.

TEARFULNESS

There is no doubt that many verbal interchanges end in tears or tearfulness.

That is because words are powerful. Words are like arrows or bullets. Bullies and dictators know only too well how to use words to best and worst effect.

Parents complain that the tears of their children – even their grown-up children – are "crocodile tears". But that assertion is very difficult to prove. You can cry without actually shedding tears. Hence the value of paper tissues.

At first, it appears the tissue is being held to wipe off perspiration or a cosmetic. Maybe your respondent is genuinely upset. In that case, is it time to be more conciliatory?

OPEN LIPS

A popular choral response is: "Open thou our lips, and our mouths shall show forth praise."

How would people react – I wonder – if the lips were opened, then nothing happened.

It is a good tease in conversation – particularly when it is impossible to get a word in edgeways – to open the lips as if to speak, then to close them again.

The onlooker merely sees a fish coming up for air.

HANGING ROUND

Nobody is entirely comfortable looking up to find somebody still in the room when that person should have left. Permission to leave has been granted, goodbyes have been said, chairs have been put back. . . but still the other person is hanging around. Why?

Lingering is invaluable. And unanswerable.

The lingering statement: "Could I just ask . . . ?" – like the exit statement – is empowering. Better still, the lingerer need say nothing.

YAWNING

Yawning is a marvellous way to interrupt somebody's dry monologue, or to draw it to a speedy conclusion.

Your yawn can be wide open, or suppressed – as long as it is evident to the talker. And that yawn can be repeated, even faked, at regular intervals.

Everybody is said to yawn at other people's holiday photographs – which is not much of a compliment to the photographer! And the Lord Mayor's "closing remarks" are scarcely more scintillating.

The yawn is a popular device because it is *instant feedback*.

THE "I" STATEMENT

Any statement beginning with "I" – such as
- "I like,"
- "I think," or
- "I am unsure,"

– has far more influence and power than a statement beginning with "You": such as
- "You are wanting. . ,"
- "You are supposing. . ." or
- "You are getting me all mixed up."

You-statements lend themselves to denial, and misunderstanding. I-statements, by contrast, are firmer and uncontestable.

ONE WORD ANSWERS

Most people do not expect one-word answers in reply to their questions. So the impact is startling when an answer is only one word.

Repliers with one word emerge with a reputation for being very learned and inscrutable. That is surprising because the opposite might be expected:

- "Do you agree that Britain might enjoy greater wealth, more prosperous commerce, and immeasurable influence on the world stage , if it enters the Single Currency?" **"Yes!"**
- "Could you describe your journey here to-night?" **"Awful!"**
- "What is the secret of traffic control?" **"Pricing."**

THE GAP

Practise the art of leaving a gap after you have made a statement. That little space – perhaps accompanied by slightly pursed chin – has enormous impact on the listener .

Talker and listener alike look expectantly at each other.

It hardly matters if your one perfectly-timed comment is not followed by any other comment.

It is *the gap* that is remembered.

PLEASE HANG ON

The best candidates at job interview leave a pregnant pause *before* embarking upon any answer. This tactic can be used on many other occasions.

There is no need to start speaking straightway when asked to relate an experience, an interest, or an opinion.

Nor is there danger that your listener(s) will lose concentration. In fact, the opposite.

Sit or stand composed. Relish the suspense. People listen harder if they have waited a little longer.

HALF WAY THERE

Try ending a tale, or ending any set of comments, *half way through*. Example: "I was out walking the dog and we came to this river. You'd never believe what happened next."

Look round at this point. Make no attempt to resume.

If you're criticizing the Government, stop at the point where you've said: "Traffic limitation looks like failing."

The impact of *not* elaborating further is to leave the other person far more eager to hear the ending.

THE STATEMENT

Make statements instead of asking questions. Try never to say anything that in writing would be followed by a question-mark.

For instance: "You look unwell," is far better than asking : "Are you unwell?"

Your listener can always ask for clarification if you are wide of the mark.

People respond better to statements than to questions – because they lose the fear of being interrogated. Nobody wants to be on the rack.

NO COMMENT

It is absolutely infuriating to hear somebody cornered saying: "No Comment!" We as listeners or viewers feel cheated. Especially when the person responding to the interviewer is an official *spokesman*. We think that such a character jolly well ought to have a comment.

Nonetheless, "No Comment!" can be an extremely useful device in everyday speech, especially when a parent is questioned by her children. There really is no answer to "No Comment."

STALLING

Stalling is not one technique but many – progressing from:
"No Comment," through: "Give me a moment," to: "Wait and see."

"Wait and see" is particularly infuriating for children, because it
leaves them mid-air.

Very clever practitioners stall by saying: "I know I am stalling [or
holding back] on that question. That is because I am awaiting. . ."
And the secret of awaiting is always to be waiting.

ARE THESE YOUR WORDS?

"Are these your words?" is a standard checking-out statement or question.

Suspicion that words are not the speaker's own might be aroused by:

- The words sounding off-pat;
- The words sounding too diplomatic;
- The words sounding borrowed;
- The words sounding like an agreed line; or
- The words sounding too impressive, or
- Too inoffensive.

The question: "Are these your words?" is a sure conversation-stopper – an unwelcome interruption.

LET ME ILLUSTRATE

Sales teams are instructed as to how a good illustration clinches a good sale. Most effective is demonstration of the product(s) for sale. Failing that, use the catalogue, or an artist's impression.

In conversation, it really does not matter whether the illustration is a chart or a graph or a scroll or a cassette tape, a doll, drug, plate or can of baked beans.

Any illustration is better than none. An ordinary pen or torch or ruler can he used to illustrate a point. The more fertile the imagination, the better the illustration. And the better the illustration, the more likely an entire conversation will be remembered.

TOYS

Maybe it is infuriating. Maybe it is naff. But an adult bringing along a child's toy to illustrate a point gets the message across. Toys are cheap and accessible.

Children use toys as role-play for later on in their lives; therefore adults are justified bringing the same toys out for recall. The great Channel Tunnel was financed through the construction of a toy-train set!

Use marbles, miniature people, model cars, plastic soldiers, Lego, cuddly animals, snow-storms, or dolls.

Brought out properly, toys are not patronizing.

LOOK AT THIS NEWSCUTTING

Newscuttings are a novel, yet inexpensive, way to illustrate a conversation or discussion. People tend to study newsclippings thoroughly, and not to question their authenticity.

Some newscuttings are hopelessly biassed; more are not.

Newscuttings are very cheap. They are also versatile. A well-chosen cutting, or clipping, can round off an argument, or take people onto the next argument.

Generally, newspapers are abandoned too easily or too quickly to the bin or to the fish-and-chip shop. Best in newspapers are their marvellous photographs and cartoons. Very few people miss out on a caption.

ARGUING FROM ONE PERSON'S ANGLE

Some of the best stories concentrate on *one particular person* rather than a whole group or tribe or country in commotion.

TV and Radio reporters are past masters at narrowing down focus to *one* family or *one* person – whether it is the Queen's first visit to a city, or a dreadful disaster.

Listeners tend to respond to one *single* person, because the problem or the delight is then far more manageable. One family flooded is easier to understand than Global Warming.

Always in conversation, show how just *one* individual – maybe yourself – has benefited or suffered.

HALF-TRUTH

A whole book could be written about the half-truth. Sometimes it is mistakenly called White Lie, or Being Economical with the Truth.

Yet *real* half-truth has no hint of dishonesty about it. The intention is not to mislead nor to make a false gain. Half-truth, at its best, is there to win time.

- "A very interesting meeting" is the half-truth for deadlock.
- "An unforgettable colleague" is the half-truth for oddball.
- "Tries his very hardest" is the half-truth for modest results.

At some point, half-truth merges with *euphemism*: the separate art of putting the best gloss on events.

There are entire dictionaries devoted to the euphemism.

OMISSION

Omission, used kindly helps other people. Omission – leaving out a large chunk of debate or information – hardly ever offends.

Omission is only culpable when it leads directly to misery: not telling another person about a missing stair or the consequence of their heavy drinking.

At other times, omission is a very good decision or outcome. If in doubt, leave out.

Omission can rarely be detected because nobody is sure what is going on inside somebody's head. Nobody is certain what *the whole* might have been.

IMITATING

Imitating isn't the same as copying. *Copying* another speaker rarely works; the device is too easily rumbled.

Imitating means picking up one or two ingredients from another person's speech: perhaps a slightly high voice, or a pregnant pause, or the odd "to be perfectly honest," and imitating those ingredients.

The best imitation is still *disguised.* Counsellors are taught to put distressed interviewees at ease by imitation.

SPEAKING IN CODE

Whenever you're faced with attentive children, or unfamiliar guests in a room, it might be necessary to speak in code.

Code has the advantage of getting a message across without revealing more than is absolutely necessary – rather like answering a barrister's searching questions in cross-examination.

The code could be as simple as: "Go ahead and collect that package and deliver it to the address we agreed," or as complex as: "The diagnosis is certainly a surprise, but the right treatment should help her somewhat."

CRACKED RECORD

Assertiveness classes have become the staple of community and adult education. One lesson taught in : "How to Be More In Control" is the Cracked Record response.

Simply say the same thing over and over again: "I'm not satisfied," "I'm not satisfied," "I'm not satisfied"; "Please leave these premises," "Please leave these premises," "Please . . .

The cracked record is especially useful if you are complaining. But the stratagem fails completely if the speaker gets flustered, or shouts.

I DISAGREE

Generally, we search for harmony most of the time. We could not live with disharmony *all* the time.

So it takes some courage to disagree, especially in a larger group where opinion is swinging in one direction only.

Even so, a simple interruption, or reply:
"I disagree!" is both dramatic and effective.

"I disagree!" needs no qualification, or even explanation.
Certainly do not say: *"I'm afraid* I disagree."

I'LL SAY THIS JUST ONCE

How often we ruin the effect of what we want to announce by announcing it over and over again within a few sentences!

Once is enough. If the listener wants to hear it again, then (s)he must make a direct request to hear it again.

It is important that you as speaker should be in the driving-seat. That involves your sounding a little injured if what you said was not picked up the first time.

I'M AFRAID I DON'T UNDERSTAND

Forget whether you understand or not. Particularly at work, or in any remotely hostile environment, practise saying: "I'm afraid I don't understand."

The original speaker – the antagonist – has no way of knowing whether you are an innocent or an artful dodger. So (s)he has to begin all over again.

Strange to recount, the original speaker isn't nearly so pig-headed or adversarial the second time round. And you have a valuable few seconds extra to collect your thoughts.

I WONDER: "COULD YOU SAY THAT AGAIN?"

This device is similar to: "I'm afraid I don't understand," but commoner. Some people say: "Come again. . ." instead of asking : "Could you say that again?" Whatever the precise wording, it is the original speaker, not the listener, who is placed on the spot having to reiterate the exact same words.

Interestingly, on repetition, these words are rarely *exactly* the same.

SAYING THE OPPOSITE

Little children love to say the opposite, just for fun. If you say: "East Coast," they say "West." If you say: "Cereals," they say "Porridge, please." Saying the opposite actually clarifies an argument as well as obstructing it.

So when you hear: "Mrs. Smith is a right old moaner," you reply: "I actually find Mrs. Smith very cheerful, considering all she's been through."

Opposites (the true meaning of *opposition*) provide greater force and focus than tame consent.

PARADOX

The idea of paradox is to suggest to somebody *the opposite of* what you want them to do or say. Then they will conform to your wish!

This tactic works because some people are very obstinate and hate to be pushed in one direction.

You can adapt paradox by **saying** the opposite of what you yourself think about a subject, in order to wheedle out the other person's true stance.

Paradox should *never* be used to cause danger.

STONEWALLING

Learn to **stonewall**. Use stonewalling, adamantly, whether in the office, in the street, or in the midst of your own family.

The beginning of stonewalling is to make very short, crisp, statements and never to divert from them.

If you are asked what you've been doing all day, say: "Paperwork." If asked for your opinion on Iraq, simply say : "It's complicated."

If pressed, again, simply say: "Leave it at that."

GOING FURTHER DOWN THE LINE

When the speaker gets to a fixed point, what better than (s)he finds the listener already further down the line?

A classic response to "Bring back hanging!" is: "For sheepstealing and shop theft." Similarly, the best response to "Give me salad, anyday!" is: "You mean salad for breakfast, lunch and tea?"

Most comments develop an absurdity of their own if taken just that bit too far down the line. Yet we rarely take the talker that second mile.

TEARING UP THE SCRIPT

A great number of conversations are already "scripted."
They run along set lines (literally) just as if taken from the theatre.

We don't always want to alter the way we interact with those who
are close to us – so we stick with what we know.

Therefore, it is quite deflating when we *tear up* someone else's
script.

Try saying: "Now let's depart from the text . . . , " or
"Forget the preamble. Keep the flowers. Get cracking."

WHAT ARE YOU TRYING TO SAY?

This interjection is about as unhelpful as possible, masked as rescue.

"What are you trying to say?" actually questions the previous speaker's clarity. It implies that there has been some muddle or waffle.

With rescue like this, who would not prefer to sink?

PERMISSION TO SPEAK

The catch-phrase in Dad's Army: "Permission to speak. . ." gained enormous acceptance not just because the request was uttered by so lovable a character, but also because those words were richly evocative of Primary School.

The standard way still to gain attention in first school is to raise the hand, one hand only. The teacher then hears each child in turn *at her direct request.*

In everyday teenage or adult conversation, "Permission to speak" is a devastating request. It tells the first speaker (s)he has been going on and on. Simply raising the hand high in the air – just as in primary school – has the same impact.

LET'S STOP JUST THERE

Three or four tactics in conversation are taken directly from the cassette tape-recorder. The audio or video cassette can normally he stopped, or paused, at any point, even halfway through a sentance or scene.

If one speaker dares to say: "Let's stop just there!" there's not a lot other persons in the room can do about it.

They are bound to stop and reflect at that exact point. The requester s, as usual, acting with audacity – so daring that it frequently succeeds. It's called *dwelling* on a point.

LET'S PLAY THAT AGAIN

"Let's play that again" is another device taken from the cassette recorder. At first, this might seem like Cracked Record – but it is not. Cracked Record is insistent, and rather confrontational.

- "Let's play that again" is a gentler form of persuasion.
- "Let's run through that argument again."
- "Let's look at that sequence [of events] again."

In other words, the most recent information or knowledge presented is so important that it would be a pity to rush straight on to the next topic or decision.

WHAT'S THE BOTTOM LINE?

"Let's cut the cackle. Let's not get bogged down in the detail at this stage. Exactly: what is the bottom line?"

Looking for a bottom line means looking for an end-result or an end-cost, or simply any ending. Then, with the ending (literally) in sight, it is much easier to face or skip the middle stages.

Obviously, you cannot ask for the bottom line straightway. That would be counter-productive. But it is handy to know bargaining limits (or consequences) fairly early on.

JOIN US

"Join us!" or "Come and join us!" are expressions much used in bars, hotels and dance halls to drag outsiders, strangers, or past acquaintances into conversation.

"Join us!" has its origins in politeness. The loner is so *feared* that it is felt to be polite to draw the loner in, to ensure everybody has a good time.

"Join us!" is a most remarkable device, because it hardly allows for refusal. There is no reply except to join, and the very act of joining is sometimes unwelcome compromise.

FORBIDDEN SUBJECT

Children are understandably curious – and furious! – when they hear that a subject is forbidden. Adults are not much happier either. We should like *every* subject to be open to debate and disagreement.

Subjects are forbidden for many reasons: delicacy, decency, confidentiality, irrelevance, timing, policy, or in order to combat oppression (racism, sexism, ageism etc.).

It does not take much imagination to work out that it is *highly convenient* for certain subjects to be out of bounds. Moreover, almost anybody can declare a subject forbidden, without giving a reason.

DELIBERATELY RAISING A FORBIDDEN SUBJECT

Just as subjects can be declared *forbidden* quite arbitrarily, so forbidden subjects can be raised without notice.

That is because nobody can control what is going on in another person's head, nor what reaches that person's lips. The listener or defendant or adversary might relish (or rely upon) a forbidden subject being aired.

In fact, declaring a subject forbidden [as opposed to assuming that it is not for discussion] can provoke people to raise it.

And it is always possible to slip one subject in beneath another.

DRONING

It is possible to make an impact by deliberately droning on and on and on, in monotones.

Perhaps you want to put somebody off the scent; or else you want to voice an apology, but not too abjectly.

Droning is effective getting rid of somebody – probably the same somebody who was relentlessly boring on a previous occasion.

Finally, droning always works when telling good news or glad tidings. The listener then grows *more* interested.

GREAT GRATITUDE

Gratitude is one thing; great gratitude is another.

Everybody likes a word of thanks where thankfulness is appropriate.

Should however that gratitude overflow into great gushes, it becomes an embarrassment and a mockery.

Gratitude is wonderful. . . because it can be turned on *instantly*.

GREAT SERVILITY

People used to sign letters with such inconsequentials as: "Yours Obligingly," or "Your Obedient Servant."

There has always been a whiff of mockery, not to say exaggeration, about servility.

Of all respectfulness, obsequiousness is the least reliable constituent. We all remember figures like Uriah Heap who overdid their fawning to the point of slavish grovelling.

Use: "Yes Sir! No Sir! Three Bags Full, Sir!" very sparingly.

EXAGGERATING ASSENT

Any exaggerated behaviour is suspect. Yet exaggerating assent is a popular and completely acceptable gesture. We all want to be agreed with. It is a compliment to be agreed with.

Some listeners hum or purr to express assent. But at times the hummers or the purrers overdo it.

But how is this to be rumbled? The agree-er is urging the speaker on to say more. The speaker rambles on delighted (s)he has hit the right note or found a soul-mate.

FALSE ANGER

One tool of the trade senior managers are taught is to be angry when they are not truly angry.

Several parents adopt the same strategy – then chuckle when their naughty child has fled.

False anger has the advantage of sounding rather like true anger – especially from a partner or parent or manager one has not seen in that state before.

False anger is also **more restrained** than genuine, uncontrolled, anger – so it hits its target with more dignity.

Use rarely.

FALSE CONFIDENTIALITY

The line between confidentiality and false confidentiality is extremely slender.

In soap operas, the audience knows that the woman entrusted with the most secrets is also the most unreliable receptacle for those precious secrets.

Nonetheless, it is easy to be sucked in by leaking buckets who turn their ears closest to the conversationalist, a bit too sure that: "You can tell me."

False confidentiality includes making *unimportant* observations and revelations sound momentous.

FALSE PRECISION

Many decisions in life rely upon precision. A good example is mortgage interest rate. "About 7%" is not good enough for a loan of £80000. Similarly, a train leaves at 18-18 , not "round 6-30pm."

Yet there are times precision is neither required nor expected in conversation. Thus, *false precision* will have the advantage, or disadvantage, of highlighting one bit of any discussion: "She is $51^1/_2$ years old," or "I stood 63 feet away to take that photograph," or: "Please buy 41 ounces."

False precision is sometimes occasion for a joke – but make sure not to be remembered as a pedant.

FALSE PREMISE

If the foundation block is wrong, all that is built on that foundation is probably wrong as well.

Listeners catch onto an accurate premise, for instance:
- "Because supermarkets have huge buying power, they can buy and sell goods cheaper."

But the same premise could lead to a ridiculous statement:
- "Because supermarkets have huge buying power, they are obliged to trade responsibly."

Equally, that premise could be changed, and *still* be wrong:
- "Because supermarkets have shareholders, they trade responsibly."

Always query foundations.

QUOTATION

Quotations can be trite and repetitive additions to speech or conversation, but they are surprisingly effective.

A quotation is either mugged up or produced spontaneously:
- "Comment is free; fact is sacred";
- "I must go down to the sea again."

A quotation can also be a pun: "Neither borrower nor blender be."

Any quotation aptly and cleverly chosen can make a speaker sound more authentic.

An attributed quotation: *"E. W. Rogers said: Ask a p'liceman"* is even more impressive.

MISQUOTATION

Misquotation is irritating and unfunny unless the speaker makes it quite plain that (s)he is spinning a yarn or making a joke.

"She came; she saw; she conquered" – would offend few.

But: "I promise to speak the truth, the whole truth, and everything except the truth," sounds slick and cynical.

The more remote the quotation, eg. "A traveller from the cradle to the grave" (Shelley), the more it falls on the user to get it right.

DEMANDING DEFINITION

If you are bored with what is being said, or if you do not respect the questioner, demanding definition can be an effective sidetrack.
- "Negligence" is a good word to ask to be defined;
- "careless" is another;
- "damaging"allows plenty of debate;
- "cause" can be endlessly discussed . . . and so on.

Some definitions are essential, but others like "a good meal," or "an unhappy ending" have to be taken as read in order to prevent a conversation becoming bitty, or pedantic.

SLIPPING IN A DODGY STATEMENT

The story goes that in "The Times" one hundred or so years ago an extremely long – and boring – speech was reprinted in tiny type. Into the heart of this screed was inserted a crude observation entirely alien to the paper.

So it is in conversation. Whilst making many points: eg. "Lamb is too expensive, milk is too expensive, apples are too expensive. . ." it is possible to insert a dodgy statement like: "Tobacco is too expensive."

If the audience has been lulled into accepting sense, the reasoning goes they will accept a dose of nonsense.

CONSIDER THESE POINTS

If you are busy arguing that too few privately-rented bedsits have proper hot water, the last thing you want to hear is that some lukewarm water is available at 6-30am.

Similarly, if you are arguing that computers are far too expensive, you are confused to hear that one shop has reduced the most popular model from £1100 to £1050. There are middle stages between all extremes, but those middle points are irrelevant when your sole intention is to flag up folly, exploitation or lawbreaking.

You cannot be half a thief or half a churchgoer. So do not trouble to quibble over minor or feeble concessions.

SPLIT THE DIFFERENCE

It might be sensible to meet halfway when faced with a long journey – but it is certainly not so wise to meet halfway in an argument.

For instance, Dad offers Alan £ 3 pocket money. Alan holds out for six pounds. The answer is **not** £4-50, split the difference, particularly when Dad is on Income Support. The answer is £ 3.

Similarly, one person wants speeding restricted to 20mph in heavily built-up areas; an opponent is content with 40. A solution is not the age-old 30mph.

The middle way should apply only to more complex debates. Most days, halfway is another trick.

CHOOSE JUST ONE

- "It's Skegness, or nowhere!"
- "Five pounds an hour, or don't trouble me further."
- "England in May is either roasting or bitterly cold."

All three examples here are *extremes*.

The respondent is expected to choose, or to accept, just one extreme. No mention is made of alternative extremes, or alternative choices between stated extremes.

Polar points are a deceit, if only because the further away you get, the nearer you get to where you started.

Very few issues are resolved **all** or **nothing**, start or finish, ardent belief or complete disbelief.

I'M WANTING TO RESTRICT MYSELF

Beware of anybody who starts a sentence:
- "I'll restrict myself to . . . " or:
- "To-day, I'll talk only about . . . "

This self-limitation aids clarity and direction, but the choice of topic is very much the speaker's not the listener's.

If you want to know somebody's views about punishment, it is really no help if you get a reply covering only imprisonment. If you want to know about building permission in two years' time, reference to building permits *already* granted is only half an answer.

I DON'T EXPECT . . .

- " I don't expect an answer to-day."
- "I don't expect a positive response to my invitation."
- "I don't expect you will agree with me."
- "I don't expect Sally will go along with us."

All "**I don't expect**" statements are highly speculative, and rarely verifiable.

"I don't expect" is bold presumption (or assumption).

"I don't expect" is a piece of bait.

BOUNCING

None of us like to be "bounced" into making up our minds – but this tactic is used all too often to unsettle us, or to get us to buy something quickly:

- "What have you to say about this?"
- "I've received this complaint about you and I have to reply straightway."
- "Buy now and save 40% on the listed price."
- "We must all reach a decision within 5 minutes."

Now is a horrible tactic, made worse by the fact that the option is rarely given to go away and think about it, or to prepare a proper reply with all the facts to hand.

Therefore, *insist* on more time.

BY THAT I MEAN

Most words do not have a completely obvious meaning:
- **"Fruit"** can mean everything from a tomato to a grape;
- **"Christian"** can mean Methodist or Mormon;
- **"Best-seller"** can mean a book that has sold 2000 or one that has sold 2 million copies.

Some of life's cleverest talkers artificially limit themselves to the meaning that illustrates their argument best of all.

It is much easier to talk about torture when punishment beatings are not included. More sympathy is gained condemning yobs than errant girls.

NOBODY WOULD DISAGREE

Politicians love the affirmation: "Nobody would disagree," for obvious reasons.

It lulls the audience to sleep. It gives each listener a false sense of security that *at last* common ground has been reached [an illusion].

What "nobody disagrees with" is often highly contentious.
In fact, there are remarkably few propositions in life that *nobody at all* would disagree with.

MY RELIGION STATES

We do not live in an especially religious era; but the absence of strong religious observance opens the door to all religious beliefs – however off-beat, or sectarian. . . particularly now the Millennium is here.

Coming from a priest: "My religion states" is a defensible. Coming from a known adherent: "My religion states" is understandable. It has a context.

But dragged in by anybody, any time, "My religion states. . ." is merely ingenious (and completely beyond contradiction).

WORSE EVILS

Just start talking about betting and the other person speaks of match-fixing as *a worse evil*. Just start talking about double-glazing, and the reply centres on *the greater evil* of selling timeshare accommodation overseas.

Worse evils are essentially *distractions*. Attention should be given to the first anomaly, the first injustice, before jumping to consider the second.

All too true in conversation: two wrongs do not make a right.

SPECULATION

People are constantly trapped by idle speculation . . . because they are never certain that it is speculative. Newspapers are full of what a prince or princess does or does not think.

Nobody, absolutely nobody except that royal, could ever know for sure. Even on points of fact, or supposed fact, a lot of chatter is pure speculation :
- "Marie wants another four babies;"
- "The only reason they're moving home is mortgage arrears"; or
- "The year after next will see substantial tax increases."

Anybody can speculate without letting their listener(s) know they are speculating. And it all sounds so convincing.

HERE IS THE PROOF

We all love proof. Proof gives us a sense of triumph, victory. The temptation is to believe that nobody will ever argue with proof: especially a complex statistic.

Hold up a blown tin of outdated corned beef :
     "Here is proof that Britain's food safety does not work."
The can is no proof whatsoever, except possibly that one store has got its stock-control hopelessly wrong.

A 30% exam mark is no proof of a child's idleness. (S)he could have been ill; the exam paper could have been poorly written; or the examiner could have been too strict.

Proof is in the speaker's, not the hearer's mind. Very cunning.

TRUE STATISTIC

People love a statistic. So a statistic – or rather a clutch of statistics – is exactly what they get.

Everyone half knows that each statistic is open to interpretation, but the statistical medicine still goes down amazingly well.
- "Half of all people are unable to preset their videos";
- "More unmarried couples separate than married couples";
- "20% of children eat no fresh fruit or vegetables" –

each of these statements is statistically true.

Statistics well-used enrich an argument.

FALSE STATISTICS

It is remarkably easy to slip a false statistic into a debate, especially if the speaker sounds convincing.

Listeners are never sure whether the authoritative one is right or wrong. Checking up takes too long.

- "Four-fifths of advertizing improves sales.";
- "Doctors say a third of all women may benefit.";
- "Air traffic will rise by 77% before 2009." –

Even if all these figures are wrong, nobody *intended* to deceive. We hope. False statistics are everywhere.

TECHNICAL JARGON

You don't have to be talking to a scientist or a mathematician to be confused by jargon. Each profession, including professions in direct contact with the public – such as nursing and social work, has its own abbreviations and circumlocutions:

- "Injured Combat Personnel" are wounded soldiers.
- "R.I.C.s" are children received into Care.
- "Sitting *in camera*" means sitting in private.

In everyday conversation, unnecessary or obscure jargon should either be challenged, or else deployed in order to confuse.

WITHOUT DOUBT . . .

"Without doubt. . ." – or better still: "Without *any* doubt" is an excellent way to mislead your listener(s).

There probably *is* a great deal of doubt surrounding what you have said, or what you are about to say. But because you introduce the topic as being beyond reasonable unbelief, you place the other person(s) in the unenviable position of having to refute the irrefutable.

THE FISHING TRIP

Nearly every child, nearly every conversationalist, and nearly every interviewee is caught out by the fishing-trip :
- "Perhaps you'd like to tell me more about . . ." or
- "I noticed two packets were missing," or:
- "You are obviously very anti-Police."

The individual being talked to can probably say no more about the first subject; is entirely unaware that any packet is missing; indeed, is fairly *pro*-Police.

The aim of every fishing expedition is for the speaker to find out more than would ever have been volunteered. So, words are put in the listener's mouth.

THAT IS NOT WHAT X WOULD SAY . . .

To say:
- "That is not what your wife would say. . ," or
- "That is not what your employer would say. . ," or
- "That is not what X would say if (s)he were here. . ."

is to put a speaker so firmly in his or her place as to make further progress almost impossible.

As so often when employing simple conversation-stoppers, there is no *measure* of truthfulness or reliability.

Nobody knows what spouse or associate or employer would have said in that situation; therefore, it is all a happy hunting-ground.

PERSONALIZING AN ISSUE

Part of the art of personalizing an issue is remembering what it was like for you.

So if theft is being discussed, what was it like to be the victim of stealing? If money is an issue, what was it like to be short of money?

Personalizing anything brings it into focus.
People are better looking at a single painting than a gallery; at a single can than a cannery.

On the other hand, personalizing remote (or academic) topics can be destructive. Not everybody who raises a matter intends it to be a slight on the listener, a pointing of fingers. So: "please don't take it personally."

DEFENCE

Most people are natural defenders of their own interests and opinions. But everyone faces times when they are too afraid to enter a defence, or too tired, or too muddled.

Most positions allow some defence. If an opportunity for defence is missed, come back to it. Enter your defence belatedly. Better than not at all. Ask for another meeting or another conversation.

A handy way of defending what has already been lost is to say that *new evidence* has been uncovered.

Shaky defenders survive by being more brazen than the next person.

ATTACK

Attack is fine for theoreticals, when neither person is too bothered about a question or an outcome.

Attacking the person rather than their ideas has no excuse. Nor has attacking a notion or a finding or a report before it has been given a proper airing.

Attack (even, or especially, attack as a form of defence) leaves a bad flavour behind. Attack is demeaning to the *attacker*, and certainly to the person(s) attacked.

THIS IS A WEAKNESS

Classic marketing strategy is that a salesperson admits to a weakness in self or in the product being sold. Admitting a weakness is amazingly disarming. People being sold a car do not expect to be told that it does fewer miles to the litre. People interviewing for a job do not expect to be told by candidate X she lost a previous job through overwork, or lack of computer skills.

The key lies in only admitting something *rather trivial* or *peripheral*, leaving the bulk untouched and enticing.

YOU'LL JUST HAVE TO ACCEPT . . .

Acceptance of a person or proposition is the key to progress. So when acceptance is in doubt, it has to be commissioned.

- "You'll just have to accept. . ." is a trick.
- "You'll just have to accept me as I am," is a cop-out.

Objectionable people do *not* have to be accepted as they are. They are, capable of change. . . but resistant to it.

"You'll just have to accept. . ." is a feeble device for tranquillizing a competitor or questioner – for calming him or her down. Don't be neutralized.

GATHERING A CONSENSUS

"Let's stop at this point to gather a consensus," "to draw together everyone's opinion."

This is another brilliant device (taken from the context of formal meetings) for delay. And again, nobody can reasonably argue with stopping to gather up opinion(s).

Consensus is the direct alternative to conflict. Although conflict works well in Soap Opera or fiction, in everyday life agreement or consensus is the far better goal.

INTERRUPTION OF FLOW

Almost everything that person 2 says, or persons 3 and 4 say, in response to person 1, counts as an interruption.

The **convention** of everyday speech is that person two should wait for the right gap or pause *or invitation* before adding to the discussion. Additions need permission because conversations cannot make sense unless their flow is maintained.

Interrupting flow is sometimes called butting in; two people speaking at once; or miscueing.

Some (unpopular) people are deliberate, unreformed, interrupters – like the radio interviewers of prominent politicians.

INTERRUPTION OF CONTENT

Interruption of content is, by definition, also an interruption of flow.

- "Could we move on to discussing animals?" or
- "Do we also have the price of wheat to hand?" or
- "There is the matter of Farm Subsidies to raise. . ." –

are all interruptions *of the content* of an agricultural discussion. The same can apply to the content of any area of debate.

By raising any one issue, open house is invited on all linked or unlinked issues. Persons who enjoy diversions will only stop if slapped down or fobbed off. It's a cruel world.

TIRESOME DETAIL

Probably the most hated of all interrupters or listeners is the person attached to tiresome or irrelevant detail.

Say you are explaining the price of clothes in Debenhams, it is irritating to be asked whether to go to floor three or floor four. If you are marvelling at the wonders of steam locomotives on preserved lines, it is infuriating to be asked whether the engine is made in Leeds or in Derby. A good anecdote does not mean more if a child is 7 or 8 years old, or if Birmingham is 110 or exactly 100 miles away.

Naturally, a *welter* of tiresome detail can catch somebody off-guard at the moment of *essential* detail.

RESERVING JUDGEMENT

Whenever anything happens on T.V., or in court, or around psychology, a *watered down* version filters down into the public consciousness.

This is especially true of famous catch-phrases like: "Rhubarb!" or "Didn't she do well?"

From the Law Lords – of all places – comes the Reserved Judgement. That involves a judge or a bench being asked to reach a judgement but running out of time to do it properly. Judgement will be given at a much later date.

Imaginatively, reserving judgement can be used in everyday speech too. A marvellous way to sit on the fence.
And the later date does not always materialize.

I'LL BEAR THAT IN MIND

"I'll bear that in mind," is the perfect ending to any discussion, especially one that has lacked harmony.

"I'll bear that in mind," means very little, and should never be taken as a guarantee of future good conduct, future offerings.

"I'll bear that in mind," is not even an admission of responsibility for anything *not* borne in mind during the past.

LEAVE THAT WITH ME

"Leave that with me. . ." is a classic **wait-and-see** statement. It is a fob. Me is the worst place where something should be left!

There is absolutely no assurance that anything will be done at any time to further your cause or your interest.

You could be leaving a decision or an outcome forever.

Administrators say instead: "Let's put that in the pending basket." Judges say: "Let's reserve judgement."

I SHOULD LIKE TO, BUT . . .

Fobs or consolations are so common in everyday speech that too little attention is paid to them.

Akin to
- "Circumstances conspire to. . ," and
- "If only time allowed. . ," is:
- "I should really like to, but."

This apology can be concluded in any fashion:
- ". . .but there are more pressing matters,"
- "but I'm not allowed," or
- "but money has run out."

The **but** is so expected that the "I should really like to" is redundant.

I WONDER, COULD WE DRAW TO A CLOSE?

This is the chairman's finest tool:
> "I wonder, could we (perhaps) draw to a close?"

It is a very polite way of saying that enough is enough. Discussion has been allowed, allowed to circulate, allowed even to gallop away. Now is the moment to reach some conclusion.

This tool can be used even when there is *no* strict time limit.

[A version of this tactic is: "Let me just summarize . . . " Selectively.]

EXIT

A classic technique in conversation or interview is to leave the most important – or else the most damning – statement until the very end: the point of actually making one's exit.

In counselling, counsellors are told to watch out for the off- loader-at-the-door. In a way, it is *safest* to say what you truly wanted to say at the point of no return.

A word of reassurance, or a pearl of wisdom, can also best be left to the bitter end.

Soap operas on T.V. ritually make exit-statements the most cutting or nail-biting.

FLIRTATION

This device speaks for itself. That is its power.

Nobody is quite sure what flirtation is, but they know it when they have seen it. It could be flirtation is merely a male creation to boost the male ego; more likely it downgrades women in the workplace. – when taken too far.

Flirting encompasses: Winking, Smiling, Coyness, Coquetry, Demureness, Reticence, Pouting, Sexiness, False Modesty, Enticing Voice, Rapid Apology, Bashfulness, Heavy Eye Make-up, Scanty Dress and Purring.

If flirting is flirted with, it is most effective when *un*self-conscious.

SEARCHING

If you are a past expert in the art of distraction or distractability, there is no better way of interrupting the flow or the meaning of anything that is being said than to start *searching*.

You could search for a ticket, a visiting card, a coin, or an imaginary pen. If the searcher is wearing jacket, trousers and anorak: all the better. That gives at least 13 different pockets to search in!

The non-searcher is hardly in a position to call off the search.

MAKING A DRAMA

Most happenings in life have startlingly dramatic content. That means they could be re-enacted on stage or screen and still excite interest or merriment.

Mending a washing machine, reversing a car, mowing a lawn, stacking a warehouse: these are all examples of *essentially mundane* activities where **how** it is done matters far more than *what* is done.

Writers of comedy are all too aware of funny potential. . . everywhere.

Describing a past incident dramatically is the essence of anecdote. But remember: the audience must be willing.

MELODRAMA

Melodrama is different from drama, and a lot more wearing. In melodrama, the unexceptional is presented as exceptional; and small sequences are described as great crises.

Melodrama is the stuff of all soap-operas. Without a hook to get the viewer to stay tuned, scenes would get duller and less engaging.

In ordinary conversation, melodrama should be used extremely sparingly. Overuse alienates listeners and makes it impossible to re-tell interesting scenes, because all possible tension has already been squeezed out or exhausted.

FANCY DRESS

A variation on wearing uniform or dignified formal dress [even outrageously informal dress] is to wear fancy dress.

The excuse – if excuse be needed – is that the wearer is on the way to another party or appointment. Fancy dress is the classic way to lighten a leaden atmosphere, or to exploit the vital element of **surprise** in conversation.

Fancy dress includes penguin suit, pyjamas, ballet dress, or army camouflage. If the wearer can carry the pretence, also the incumbant responsibility, it is essential that the fancy dress is smart and not lewd.

Many kissograms, Tarzangrams, and the like, have proved merely offensive.

CHANGE OF CLOTHING

Whatever a person is wearing at *the start* of a talk or an interview we expect that person to be wearing at the end. Or do we?

Changes of clothing are accepted, if not acceptable, during the course of a discussion.

A man can take off his jacket and/or his tie – whether invited to or not. A woman can slip off her cardigan, or even her shoes. The other person(s) in the room might be too surprised to say anything!

If there is a response, merely say:
"I'm hot," or – truthfully – " I need to be comfortable."

UNIFORM

For reasons largely unfathomed, wearing a uniform changes the course of a discussion or debate. The uniform can be quite humble: such as a nurse's blue checked dress, a child's maroon school blazer, or a park-keeper's flat cap.

That uniform gives added credence to whatever is being said. The uniform may even be invented. There is no law against wearing uniforms appropriate to other jobs or professions so long as nobody is hurt or deceived.

People in trains tend to avoid priests and the military.

KEEP YOUR HAT ON

One of the conventions of Victorian or Edwardian England, when hats were far commoner, was that a man especially took off his hat when talking to another man or woman.

The hat is a special item of clothing because it covers the temple and the brain. It also covers part of the face.

You can surprise many people by wearing a hat *all through* conversation or discussion.

This comes as a useful reminder of status; additionally it is a prompt to the other person(s) present not to go on too long!

Try wearing a vaguely silly hat, or an inappropriate hat – where your self-mockery will not be immediately apparent.

BOOK IN HAND

Arriving to talk book-in-hand looks extremely impressive.

And because each book can be bound in gift-wrap or plain brown paper, the listener or the audience need never know what the book contains, or even what it is called.

Some of the best books-in-hand are never actually opened. They exist for ornament only! But it always *looks as if* the book will be opened.

Try a large atlas, especially when discussing world affairs.

FILE IN HAND

Carrying a file is also very impressive. It can be a ring binder, or an expanding file.

But best of all is the envelope file, or document wallet. Files, like brief-cases, *look* authoritative.

Files are a signal that the carrier has prepared for a conversation or an interview thoroughly.

Additionally, a file makes it look as if the central person has just come from another home or office or shop or setting therefore will be using this display file to separate the new contact from all that went before.

Again, the file does not actually have to be opened.

SIGNING THE RECORD

Signing the record is a splendid way to end a discussion or a conversation. This device has been used routinely for business meetings or sales meetings since time immemorial. Less often is it used for informal or one-to-one situations.

Signing the record could depend on note-taking throughout, but there is no harm in writing a concluding note, or even a retrospective record, so long as both parties or all parties sign it.

Then, if there is later disagreement about what was or was not decided, that can be clarified. . . always provided no signature was obtained under duress.

TAPE-RECORDER IN HAND

One of the most stringent conventions of the informal meeting, interview or conversation is that proceedings will **not** be taped.

Modern technology is, however, so advanced that it is now more possible than ever before to tape, or even to film, a conversation without the other person(s) knowing. In turn, this violates another taboo : bugging or spying.

Pretending that taping is an open and legitimate objective, and actually setting out the tape-recorder, challenges the respondent to agree to its employment; also to suggest the destination (circulation) of the eventual full tape.

Opinion is divided as to whether taping alters deliberations so recorded.

LETTER OF INTRODUCTION

A fairly ancient form of etiquette was to be formally announced on entry to see somebody new. In Victorian and Edwardian times in particular, this ushering was preceded, or else accompanied, by a letter of introduction.

The letter of introduction laid out a person's credentials and the reason(s) behind that intended visit.

Occasionally, the same letter of introduction interceded on the visitor's behalf. A fragment or relic of this procedure lingers on in Court with sealed letter to the Bench.

But there is no reason not to write these letters *in*formally before a difficult conversation.

I'LL JUST WRITE THAT DOWN

Conversation is all about throwing the other person off balance or off-task or off the trail – especially where a discussion is likely to turn hostile or disappointing.

Ironically, one of the unwritten rules of many discussions is that nothing will be written down. But it is a human right that writing down *should* be allowed, especially for the weaker party or defendant.

Writing down upsets the other person(s), because nobody but the writer is entirely sure *what* has been written down; or where the notes or transcript might end up!

Contemporary notes are usually admissible in court or tribunal. Sign and date them, in any case.

POINTS IN A DIARY

The diary is a useful notebook as well as an essential reminder of appointments or commitments.

The diary is also an unobtrusive item to have in the hand or on the desk during any meeting or discussion.

If points cannot be listed on the actual date-page when they will be retrieved, arguments can be listed on quiet days like Saturdays or holidays, or on the cash page, or notes page.

The diary itself is far more accessible than a flimsy notebook.

POINTS ON A CARD

Public speakers put their main points on a piece of card or cardboard (not paper). There is no reason why private speakers, negotiators, or family members, should not also commit their themes or points to card. Card does not get lost so easily in a pocket or book or bag. The card can be a Christmas card, filing card, or postcard.

Never put down too many points. Seven links or arguments (one or two weaker ones kept in reserve!) are the absolute maximum, unless your argument is extremely technical.

REHEARSAL IN BED

Bed is a useful place to rehearse what to say and how to react to what the other people will say.

Bed is a safe environment. It is extremely private. Bed is also the place the speaker is likely to be late on the night before, or early on the same day that speaking up is really essential.

It does not matter if a speaker drops asleep still rehearsing. Waiting for a big occasion will *usually* be wakeful. Get to associate bed with theatre.

REHEARSAL IN THE MIRROR

Before any interview, or any important demand on another person's time and attention, it is rewarding to rehearse in front of a mirror.

This is even more important in advance of a confrontation.

Words do not have to be learnt off by heart, simply the gist of what will be said, or the three main points.

The mirror adds confidence to the final performance.

The first time a mirror is used, the main speaker/requester will blurt everything out immediately after entering the room. With practice, that sense of hurry soon disappears.

COULD WE ADJOURN?

Adjournments are an essential consequence of business meetings and parliamentary proceedings. Without adjournments, there is no chance for some matters to be carried forward. Discussion would go on all night – and frequently does.

Good discipline in everyday conversation also is to seek or even to call for an adjournment. That allows each person or party to consult elsewhere, and to gather further information/impressions/opinions.

Adjournments also allow antagonists to calm down. It is amazing how the atmosphere is *never identical* when conversations re-commence.

I'M SORRY I'LL BE AWAY

We are all born with a good idea of presence, and the importance of being present. What we often lack is a sense of *absence*, and the importance of being absent.

Giving apology in advance for absence means that much awaiting discussion (or decision) has to be postponed even longer. After all, in some circumstances your absence matters more than your presence.

Absence is a type of protest, or playing for time. Never over-use absenteeism. If possible, never go into detail about its cause.

SILLY OBJECT

Introducing a silly object is rather different from wearing a mask (masquerading) or using toys (instruction). The silly object does, however, have to be introduced with the same great care and forethought.

It must also contain *the possibility* that it might be for real, completely serious.

A coal scuttle can be brought into a conversation about fuel; a framed photograph into a conversation about people not present; or a tiger place-mat into a conversation about wild life. The silly object must imitate relevance.

If the bringer of silly object *is* rumbled, there is still much light-heartedness to be enjoyed.

LET'S GET A THIRD PERSON . . .

Drawing in a third person is like having an umpire at a chess match or a wrestling bout.

It is recognition by two people locked in discussion or disagreement, that they would benefit from a third person sitting in.

The snag is: it is open to *just one* of two people involved to request a third – or in the case of a group at odds with each other, it is open to just one of the group to request a facilitator.

Even if the request is turned down, it *has been requested* – and refusal looks distinctly churlish.

LET'S FIX A TIME

Every Government Department – or Local Authority – knows how vital postponement is. Postponement is the more palatable alternative to abandonment.

So the suggestion: "Let's fix a time," or
"Let's fix *another* time," is not as helpful as it sounds.

Fixing another time gives the dissident or adversary much-needed breathing time. The battle is so much easier second-time round: new day, new approach.

SLURP

An amazing number of meetings and discussions take place in settings where cold or hot drinks are available.

Drink and talk are associated – even in quite formal settings like a business meeting or an interview – because talking *by itself* is considered too delicate or demanding to be undertaken without lubrication.

Given that drink is on hand, or in hand, it is understandable that some people deliberately slurp their drink, or drink too quickly, and burp, in order to disrupt the conversation.

Even without these unwelcome distractions, drink itself is a distraction: "Coffee or tea? Black or white? With or without sugar? Large cup or small?. . ." and so on. Try *refusing* drink when talking.

WHERE IS THE CLOAKROOM PLEASE?

Nobody at all can prove whether somebody needs the loo or not. No teacher, no doctor, no inquisitor.

Therefore the simple question: "Where is the cloakroom [lavatory] please?" gets the desired response of a welcome break in the proceedings: whether a job interview, a discussion, or a fierce argument.

Things are never quite the same again after the break.

I'LL JUST RING UP

It does not really matter *whom* you say you will ring provided you *promise* to ring somebody up:
- to check a fact,
- to confirm a time, or
- to register a complaint.

It gives immediate credibility to your argument or your persistence if you intend to follow up a conversation (or episode) with that one – unheard – phone call.

ONLY TELEPHONING

Until video-phones and video-conferencing are commoner, most telephones will be impersonal voice-only machines. As such, telephoning is often simpler and more detached than meeting somebody face-to-face.

People talk a bit more freely on the telephone; and test other people's ideas without the interference of desks, coffee, doors, furniture, strangers, or the like.

Many a hard choice or decision is made on the telephone. Often, a meeting *never* happens because of the preceding call or calls.

ONLY WRITING LETTERS

Just as some people use telephones more freely than face-to face discussion, so other people find letter-writing simpler and more convenient than face-to-face meetings.

Letter-writing is also safer. More can be said in a letter ; or can be said in a different way; or can be said, then thrown in the bin, then said again.

There are even tales of people waylaying the postman in order to retrieve regretted letters.

Letter-writing can also be *unsafer* than a meeting, because a letter can be kept and shown to absolutely anyone.

PHOTOGRAPHING

If there's anything more likely than a tape-recorder to strike terror into an adversary, it is a camera. The appearance of *an unloaded* camera is sufficient deterrent to conversation. That is why some motorists always carry a camera with them.

In an age of digital and computerized photography, the photograph *does* sometimes lie. Nevertheless, an old-fashioned camera-shot is still fairly powerful ammunition.

"Can I take a photograph before leaving?" is a hard request to refuse.

TALKING TO THE TELEVISION

Answer the television – or radio – back , as if in conversation with the machine. This is all ideal preparation for answering *people* back, when the occasion demands. [Additionally, it makes for good interactive broadcasting!]

For some reason which I do not understand, it is very *uncommon* for people to answer their announcers and presenters back.

Is it because they speak with authority? Is it because they must have researched their material well?

Or is it embarrassing to reply to such an inanimate object?

FEEDBACK

Give constant feedback to the person(s) you are engaging with. Sometimes this will be verbal, some words of disappointment or appreciation. Sometimes the feedback will be non-verbal like shrugging the shoulders or rolling up the tie.

Feedback need not be during the actual meeting. It can come at the start of the next meeting:
"I did find our last session helpful."

We are often embarrassed giving or receiving *instant* feedback.

We are perhaps more used to silence, grudge, stewing – or fuming. Help to complete "the feedback loop." That way, everyone benefits.

COMPREHENSIVE INDEX

entries in brackets [-] are secondary, to assist your search.

213

INDEX BY INTENTION

(N.B. all these categories overlap)

IF ANY READER CAN THINK OF EXTRA TACTICS OR STRATEGIES FOR EVERYDAY CONVERSATION PLEASE SEND THEM TO THE AUTHOR WHO WILL GLADLY INCLUDE THEM IN A FUTURE EDITION OF THIS BOOK.

SUGGESTIONS FOR FURTHER READING

Many of the best books on the subject of talking are now out-of-print, but can easily be found in libraries or second-hand Bookshops. Here I group suggested further reading *by line of enquiry*:

For **Body Language**: The Pocket Guide to Manwatching, by Desmond Morris, Granada/Triad, 1982; Body Language, by Alan Pease, Sheldon, 1997 etc.

For **Logic**: Straight and Crooked Thinking, by Robert H.Thouless, Pan, 1964 (or any of the standard introduction to Logic). Also books by Edward de Bono, pub by Penguin.

For **Counselling**: Practical Counselling and Helping, by Philip Bernard, Routledge, 1999; Time-Limited Counselling, by Colin Feltham, Sage, 1997; or any beginner's guide.

For **Assertiveness**: Saying No ! by Asha Philips, Faber, 1999; Safe, Strong and Streetwise, by Helen Benedict, Hodder, 1997; Same Again, by M. Grant, Penguin, 1984.

For **Public Speaking**: A Guide to Public Speaking, by Robert S. Lawrence, Pan, 1963 – or any standard handbook on the subject.

For **Social Psychology**: Techniques of Persuasion, by J.A.C.Brown, Penguin, 1963; The Psychology of Interpersonal Behaviour, by Michael Argyle, Penguin, 1972; and various guides to groups and groupwork.

For **Words**: The Complete Plain Words, by Sir Ernest Gowers, Penguin 1964 and since ; Teach Yourself to Express Yourself, by R.W. Jepson, E.U.P., 1958; and, Usage and Abusage, by Eric Partridge, Penguin 1969, and since.

For **Friction**: How to Complain, by Colin Ward, Pan,1976; Stop Arguing and Start Talking, by Susan Quilliam, Vermilion, 1998 ; Bullying at Work, by Andrea Adams, Virago, 1992 ; and Couples in Crisis, by Chris Belshaw & Michael Strutt, Gollancz, 1984.

Other Very Good Books on Conversation:
What Can I Say? Finding the Right Words in Difficult Situations, by Sheila Dainow, Piatkus, 1999.

Making the Most of Yourself, by Gill Cox and Sheila Dainow, Sheldon, 1985.

Dealing With Difficult People, Robert Cava, Piatkus, 1998.

Talking With Confidence, Don Gabor, Sheldon, 1999.

How to Start a Conversation and Make Friends, Don Gabor, Sheldon, 1997.
How Conversation Works, Ronald Wardhaugh, Blackwell, 1985.
and part of British Telecom's TALKWORKS initiative: TalkWorks : How to get more out of life through better conversations, by Andrew Bailey, B.T., 1997.

+ + + + + + + + + + + +

Coming soon from

NETHERMOOR BOOKS :

Viewing it Differently

and

Through the Long Night-watches